MORE TEXAS SAYINGS

THAN YOU CAN SHAKE A STICK AT

ANNE DINGUS

ILLUSTRATIONS BY EDD PATTON

Gulf Publishing Company
Houston, Texas

Dedicated to six people who talked Texan to me:
my mother's parents,
Frederick Parker Robbins and Annabel Dodd Robbins,
and my father's sisters,
Merle Dingus, Ina L. Cowan, Rita Longbotham, and Maxie Irland.

Copyright © 1996 by Gulf Publishing Company, Houston, Texas. All rights including reproduction by photographic or electronic process and translation into other languages are fully reserved under the International Copyright Union, the Universal Copyright Convention, and the Pan-American Copyright Convention. Reproduction or use of this book in whole or in part in any manner without written permission of the publisher is strictly prohibited.

Gulf Publishing Company
Book Division
P.O. Box 2608 □ Houston, Texas 77252-2608

10   9   8   7   6   5   4   3

Printed in the United States of America.

Library of Congress Cataloging-in-Publication Data

Dingus, Anne, 1953–
    More Texas sayings than you can shake a stick at / by Anne Dingus ; illustrated by Edd Patton.
      p.   cm.
    ISBN 0-87719-292-8
    1. English language—Texas—Terms and phrases.
2. Americanisms—Texas.   3. Figures of speech.   I. Title.
PE3101.T4D56   1996
427'.9764—dc20   96-16539
                                              CIP

Introduction

Common as cornbread, old as dirt, funny as all get-out, homespun expressions link modern Texans to our rural and agricultural past, conveying the resolute spirit and plainspoken humor of our heroes and pioneers. Some sayings are instantly familiar because our parents or grandparents quoted them; others parallel the indisputable wisdom of biblical proverbs or *Poor Richard's Almanac;* plenty just make us laugh. Like blue jeans, beefsteak, and prickly pear, pithy country sayings are a Texas constant. If you enjoy them as much as I do, this book is for you; it contains a collection of sayings as big as all hell and half of Texas.

More Texas Sayings Than You Can Shake a Stick At grew from an article in the December 1994 issue of *Texas Monthly* magazine in which I presented 662 examples of great regional sayings. I spent years gleaning them from books, songs, movies, folklore, and—most of all—everyday talk. Many a friend and relative eyed me askance when, during a conversation, I suddenly dived for a pencil and jotted down a particularly nice example. Dozens of colleagues also passed on their favorites; I owe particular thanks to the witty and indispensable John Broders. Many sayings I grew up hearing are so familiar to me that I was slow to recognize them as decent material. "That's a long hard row to hoe" and "if it'd been a snake, it would've bit you" are so commonly invoked in an everyday, household context that they don't get the attention they deserve. But this kind of habitual use is what preserves the real gems.

I gleaned other Texas-isms from a plethora of sources. The books of Western lexicographer Ramon Adams remain primary reference material. The writings of legendary folklorists such as J. Frank Dobie and Mody Boatright and venerable humorists such as Alexander Sweet and Boyce House provided rich veins to mine. Various retellings of Aggie jokes and tall tales are another mother lode; we owe a lot to the spirit of Pecos Bill. You'll also find sayings aplenty in the works of many fine Texas writers, including Elmer Kelton, Dan Jenkins, Kinky Friedman, Molly Ivins, Larry L. King, and more. A nonpareil source is the script of *Greater Tuna* and its sequel *A Tuna Christmas,* written by Joe Sears, Jaston Williams, and Ed Howard. The labor of fellow sayings collectors such as Bob Bowman, Wallace Chariton, Texas Bix Bender, and others was invaluable in ensuring that I didn't overlook any classics. (Note, however, that many essential Southern and Western idioms—such as "y'all"; "fixin' to"; and "mighty," "right," and "powerful" [synonyms for "very"]—don't qualify as *sayings,* and thus do not fall under the purview of this book.)

Obviously, Texas sayings are more common in rural than in urban environments. This collection is rife with agricultural references—plows, wagons, cotton, corn, chickens, dogs, and pigs. Distinctly country references such as "clabber" and tellingly dated words like "boomtown" are common in rural sayings. Like most Texans, I learned country quips from kinfolks in small towns (Pampa, Newgulf, and Munday, in my case). But Texas expressions can be even more popular in cities. Whereas country or small-town dwellers use them out of habit and tradition, urbanites are more apt to value them as humor and folklore—a link to Texas' mythic past, to the days of the Old West, King Cotton, and Big Oil. But as warmly as Texans embrace their axioms, I confess to a few misgivings about keeping such sayings alive. Though Texas is today a largely urban and educated state, long-standing misperceptions by out-of-staters persist: Many East Coast and West Coast residents uniformly brand Texans as wild, crude, and ignorant. (It's human nature; many Texans snub Yankees in turn.) To some extent, folk sayings underscore that geographical prejudice. Ultimately, though, the inherent charm and cleverness of rural sayings overrides their potential for confirming the Texas stereotype. (And speaking of human nature, note how often the sayings gathered for a negative topic outnumber those for positive subjects. For example, I collected 47 sayings for "dumb," but only 10 for "smart.")

In Texas, the South, and the West, lawyers and politicians have always been especially enamored of the genre, often adopting a good ol' boy persona to charm juries or constituents. An aw-shucks veneer often helps to conceal a canny personality. Temple Houston, the colorful youngest child of Sam, used the phrase "he could strut sitting down" to describe self-important legal adversaries. John Nance Garner, the Uvalde-born vice president under Franklin Delano Roosevelt, once reviled that office as "not worth a pitcher of warm spit." ("Spit" was no doubt a polite substitution in published reports.) Lyndon B. Johnson once said that Liz Carpenter, Lady Bird's press secretary during his presidency, would "charge hell with a bucket of ice water." Humorist Dave Barry agreed that country sayings "are particularly effective in political rhetoric. A Southern congressman, arguing for an amendment to, say, the tax laws, will tell the U.S. House of Representatives, with a straight face, that 'you got to milk the goat before you groom the turkey,' and all the big-city Northern congressmen, not wishing to appear out of touch with The People, will nod their heads." Today attorneys and politicians help keep many gems alive. Veteran legislative counsel Patrick D. Redman supplied scores of the sayings in this book, as did many other attorneys who read *Texas Monthly*. Lawyers are especially fond of using rural expressions ironically or sarcastically; for example, "welcome as a frog in the guacamole" means "unwelcome." (In fact, every saying in the entire "Unwelcome" section begins with "welcome as . . .) And understatement is popular too: "I could sit still for that" means "you bet."

Not all of these sayings are specifically Texan. Because of the state's unique geographical position and its pivotal role in American history, Texas counts several profound cultural influences—the Deep South, the Wild West, the Mexican border, and the Midwest. However, if a Texan used it, wrote it down, quoted it, or contributed it, I counted it as a Texas saying. (This proprietary attitude toward items of nebulous origin is another traditionally Texas attitude—consider chili and rodeos.) Some sayings are regionally specific: "crazy as Larrabee's calf"; "big as Toad Denny." We can only theorize that somewhere in Texas, Farmer Larrabee had an unpredictable heifer, and that the size of said Toad Denny left an indelible impression on his neighbors. Other expressions are accessible to everyone. Among these are ubiquitous sayings like "big as Dallas" and "she looks like she's been rode hard and put away wet," as well as near-forgotten examples like "cold as a cast-iron commode" and "that about puts the rag on the bush" (which refers to the completion of housework).

Many sayings are flat-out politically incorrect. For instance, several coworkers at *Texas Monthly* pointed out that the phrases for "pretty" vastly outnumber those for "handsome." That discrepancy stems, at least in part, from the fact that most of these sayings predate our efforts to stem sexism. Using editorial license, I did, however, choose to omit racist phrases, which date from the same less enlightened era. I have also omitted several very common but indelicate sayings, and readers will no doubt call to mind coarser versions of some I did include. By the same token, I left in the occasional misuse of grammar or regional idiom. Sometimes the substitution of "don't" for "doesn't" ("he don't know a widget from a whangdoodle") or dropped "g" in an "-ing" ending ("my dogs are barkin' ") are *de rigueur* for emphasis or comic effect.

Often I was unsure to which category a particular saying belonged. "She'll tell you how the cow ate the cabbage" suggests, to some, a bossy person; to others, an angry one or, perhaps, an honest one. "Tight as Dick's hatband" means either "cheap," "drunk," or "snug," depending on the speaker and the context. Occasionally I ran across a saying that was almost impenetrable; for example, does "he was strained through a sock" mean that he's delicate, spoiled, or smelly? Some expressions demand explanation. A common weather-related remark among Panhandle residents is "there's only a strand of barbed-wire between here and there, and it's down," but unless you know that the saying refers to a severe blizzard, you're out in the cold. Therefore, to some entries in this book I have added, in editorial brackets, a brief explication or annotation. Similarly, some sayings refer to old-fashioned or outdated practices that are meaningless to many younger Texans. "It's time to put the chairs in the wagon" is a good example; it means "we've gotta go," and dates back to the nineteenth century, when relatively scarce social events drew people from miles around. Because few pioneers had a lot of furniture, families brought their own chairs, and had to pack them up when the dance or church supper was over. I occasionally added a bit of explanation for this type of saying as well. Quite a few phrases are distinctly more modern but just as pithy: "confused as a goat on Astro Turf"; "he's lost his vertical hold."

For the original article that appeared in *Texas Monthly,* art director D. J. Stout and associate art director Nancy McMillen commissioned original illustrations depicting a dozen especially vivid or popular expressions. The resulting collection, printed in the December 1994 issue, drew more response than any other article I have ever done. For months the collection made that particular magazine *Texas Monthly*'s most requested back issue. Scores of readers wrote in contributing their own favorites, and during radio interviews Texas listeners called in with dozens more. The master list grew to an amazing 1,404 sayings, covering every topic from "acceptable" to "young."

This book, with thirty-nine brand-new original illustrations by Austin artist Edd Patton, is the final product, but it is in no way complete. I have a feeling there are hundreds more that I've overlooked. Fellow admirers of the genre are invited to pass on their own contributions and comments to me at P.O. Box 1569, Austin, Texas, 78767-1569. I'd be much obliged.

Anne Dingus
Austin, Texas

Acceptable

It's better than a poke in the eye with a sharp stick.

It don't make me no never mind.

That's close enough for government work.

Might as well. Can't dance, never could sing, and it's too wet to plow.

Like a dead horse, I ain't kickin'.

I could sit still for that.

I could hold that in abeyance.

You can't beat that with a stick.

You can't beat that with a claw hammer.

Fair enough.

There you go.

Advice

See General Advice.

1

All
See Everything.

Angry
See Mad.

Arrival, Greeting

Look what the cat dragged in.

Company's coming; add a cup of water to the soup.

We've howdied but we haven't shook.

Put on your sittin' britches.

Take your hat off, but leave your boots on.

You're a sight for sore eyes.

Let's chaw the rag.

We'll rattle before we strike.

Speak of the devil!

Hello the house!

Does your dog bite? [*Can I come in?*]

Light and hitch.

The broom's behind the door. ["*Quick, company's comin'!*"]

Cool the seat of your saddle.

I'd know your hide in a tanner's shop.

I hear the thundering herd.

See also Exclamations.

Bad, Mean

He's such a liar he'd beat you senseless and tell God you fell
off a horse.

He'd see evil in the crotch of a tree.

He'd start a fight at the drop of a hat—and he'd drop it himself.

She was born sorry.

She's as sweet as a green persimmon.

Sweet as a slop jar.

So low he'd steal the widow's ax.

So low he'd steal his mama's egg money.

So low he'd steal the flowers off his grandma's grave.

So low she'd steal the nickels off a dead man's eyes.

So low he'd have to look up to see hell.

So low you couldn't put a rug under her.

So mean his mama couldn't let him nurse.

So narrow-minded he can look through a keyhole with both eyes.

He's a no-account fellow.

He's a no-good varmint.

He's a low-down dirty varmint.

He's a seven-sided SOB.

He's a real revolving SOB.

He's a spherical SOB [*that is, an SOB any way you look at him*].

She makes a hornet look cuddly.

She'll make you pray for a pine box.

A she-bear in satin.

He looks like a sheep-killing dog.

He wouldn't scratch his own mama's fleas.

He's got horns holding up his halo.

Tough as whit leather [or "*whet leather*"].

Tough as nickel steak.

Tough as stewed skunk.

Tough as whang.

He broke bad.

Bitter as gall.

Mean as a mama wasp.

Meaner than a junkyard dog.

Meaner than a wounded cougar.

Meaner than a cold snake.

Meaner than a skilletful of rattlesnakes.

"Meaner than a junkyard dog."

Friendly as a bramble bush.

Neighborly as a flea to a dog.

Rough as a cob but twice as corny.

Rougher than a stucco bathtub.

We're not on borrowing terms.

Enough to make a preacher cuss.

Born for Boot Hill.

He ain't fit to sleep with the dogs.

Hell comes for a meal wherever he hangs his hat.

She eats razor soup.

The buzzards laid him and the sun hatched him [*he had a poor upbringing*].

He could sound a sour note in a choir full of jackasses.

See also Dishonest; Mad; Unwelcome.

Beat, Conquer

He gave me the wire-brush treatment.

He's suckin' heads and peelin' tails.

He got his tail feathers trimmed.

He's been saucered and blowed.

She sure cleaned your plow.

She ran 'em around the barn.

She put the quietus on 'em.

She jumped on me with all four feet.

She walked away with the persimmons.

I got sandpapered.

I'll snatch you bald-headed.

I'll whip you like a red-headed stepchild.

I'll knock you plumb into next week.

I'll slap you into next Wednesday.

I'll hit you over the head so hard it'll break both your ankles.

I'll knock a hole in him you can throw a cat through.

I'll knock a hole in him you can see daylight through.

"If you feel froggy, you can just jump. [Wanna fight?]"

7

I'll beat you all the way to the door of death.

I'll knock your jaw so far back you'll scratch your throat with your front teeth.

If you feel froggy, you can just jump. [W*anna fight?*]

I'm gonna cloud up and rain all over you.

I'm gonna open up a whole can of whip-ass.

See also Failure.

8

Beautiful

See Pretty.

Big, Tall

Fat as a boardinghouse cat.

Fat as a town dog.

Fat as a toad.

So big he looks like he ate his brother.

**"I'm gonna open up a
whole can of whip-ass."**

So big he has to sit down in shifts.

He hasn't seen his feet in forty years.

Big as a skinned mule and twice as ugly.

Big as Brewster County.

Big as Toad Denny.

Big as Dallas.

Big as a Brahma bull.

Big as a brisket.

Big as two cords of firewood.

Big as God.

Big as all hell and half of Texas.

Bigger than outside.

Big enough to throw a cat through.

Wide as two ax handles.

She's warm in winter, shady in summer.

"Fat as a town dog."

She'd rather shake than rattle.

You don't have to shake the sheets to find her.

He'll eat anything that don't eat him first.

He don't care what you call him as long as you call him to supper.

He's big enough to bear hunt with a branch.

He's all spread out like a cold supper.

He's so tall he can't tell when his feet are cold.

His butt looks like two hams in a tow sack.

She's built tall above her corns.

She's so tall she could fix the moon without a ladder.

Tall enough to hunt geese with a garden rake.

Tall enough to catch ducks with a Crescent wrench.

These eggs are so big, it won't take many to make a dozen.

The mosquitoes here are so big, they can stand flat-footed and breed with a turkey.

Boastful

He can strut sitting down.

He's all hat and no cattle.

He's all broth and no beans.

She's all gurgle and no guts.

She's all flash and no substance.

She uses words that go eight to a pound.

He throws up too much dust.

He blows smoke—and then says it stings his eyes.

He chamber-of-commerced it.

He's shot more buck deer in that bar than any other man in Texas.

As full of wind as a corn-eating horse.

As full of smoke as a wet-wood fire.

It takes a mighty big man to weigh a ton.

See also Vain.

Braggart

See Boastful; Vain.

Brave

Timid as Tabasco.

Brave as the first man who ate an oyster.

Brave as a bigamist.

Brave enough to eat at a boomtown cafe.

He's double-backboned.

He dryholes it.

She's got more guts than you could hang on a fence.

She's full of gumption and grit.

She'd charge hell with a bucket of ice water.

She'd jump a buzz saw.

She's fearfully feisty.

He's got plenty of sand in his craw.

He'd shoot craps with the devil himself.

He'll stick to it like a june bug to a screen door.

He'd fight a rattlesnake and spot him the first bite.

He knows how to die standing up.

You couldn't stop her with forty feet of rope and a snubbing post.

Busy

He's so busy you'd think he was twins.

He's doing a land-office business.

She's jumping like water on a hot skillet.

She's got her trotting harness on.

There's no grass growing under her feet.

Busy as a one-legged man at an ass-kicking convention.

Busy as a funeral home fan in July.

Busy as a one-eyed dog in a smokehouse.

Busy as a one-armed paperhanger.

Busy as a stump-tailed bull in fly season.

Busy as a hound in flea season.

Busy as popcorn.

Busy as a frog in a hot skillet.

Busy as grease on a hot griddle.

Busy as a sackful of tomcats.

Busy as a tick in a tar barrel.

So crowded you have to go outside to change your mind.

I'm running on one foot.

I'm dealing with a passel of hassles.

I'm up to my clavicles in work [or *whatever*].

I got to slop the hogs, dig the well, and plow the south forty
before breakfast.

I got to get back to my rat killing.

Blowin' and goin'.

Many fish to fry.

Many eggs to lay.

Many bodies to bury.

A lot of dirt to scratch.

Capable, Experienced

She's got some snap in her garters.

He's got plenty of arrows in his quiver.

She's got horse sense.

She's full of mother wit.

He's got plenty of notches on his gun.

She's a right smart windmill fixer.

She keeps a weather eye out.

He knows his cans.

He could find a whisper in a whirlwind.

He knows how to cut a fat hog.

He throws a mighty wide loop.

She could swim in the air.

He can lick his weight in wildcats.

He's loaded for bear [*also means, "drunk"*].

She knows more about that than a rabbit does about running.

He don't use up all his kindling to start his fire.

He's a three-jump cowboy.

He can ride the rough string.

She's mighty thoughty [*also means "considerate"*].

If she crows, the sun is up.

He keeps his saddle oiled and his gun greased.

She'll turn on a dime and give you nine cents change.

There's no slack in her rope.

This ain't my first rodeo.

See also Smart.

Caution

You were too hard to raise to take chances.

Don't dig up more snakes than you can kill.

Whistle before you walk into a stranger's camp.

Don't plow too close to the cotton.

A dead snake can still bite.

A dead bee can still sting.

Don't tip over the outhouse.

See also General Advice.

Celebration

Let's shoot out the lights.

Let's hallelujah the county.

We'll paint the town and the front porch.

We'll go to town or at least the far pasture.

Put the little pot in the big pot.

Throw your hat over the windmill.

He's all gussied up.

I'll wear my Sunday-go-to-meeting clothes.

I'll be there with bells on.

Cheap

Tight as Dick's hatband [*also means "snug" and "drunk"*].

Tight as a tick.

Tight as a clothesline.

Tight as a fiddle string.

Tight as wallpaper.

Tight as a wet boot.

Tight as a brass brassiere.

Tight enough to raise a blister.

Tighter than two coats of paint.

Tighter than bark on a log.

Tighter than the stripe on a watermelon.

He's so tight he squeaks when he walks.

He's so tight he knows all of his pennies by name.

He'll squeeze a nickel till the buffalo hollers.

He'll squeeze a dollar till the eagle screams.

She has short arms and deep pockets.

She'd skin a flea for its hide.

She'll drive that car till the wheels are big around as doughnuts.

Citified

Raised on concrete.

Doesn't know a bit from a butt.

You don't live longer in the city; it just seems that way.

See also Dumb.

Cold

This is hog-killing weather.

There's only one strand of barbed wire between here and there, and it's down [a *blizzard reference*].

Cold as a well-digger's knee.

Cold as a frosted frog.

Cold as an ex-wife's heart.

Colder than a mother-in-law's kiss.

Cold as a cast-iron commode.

Cold as brass balls.

Cold as a banker's heart.

Cold as hell with the furnace out.

Cold as a gravestone in January.

Colder than hell on a stoker's holiday.

Cold enough to freeze ducks to the pond.

It's so cold the cows are giving milkshakes.

It's so cold I saw a dog chasing a cat, and they were both walking.

It's so cold that words are freezin'; you have to fry 'em up in a
    skillet to hear what was said.

Common

Common as pig tracks.

Common as cornbread.

Common as dirt.

Common as belly buttons.

Common as coffee.

Thick as the dew on Dixie.

Thick as fleas on a farm dog.

Thick as hops.

See also Quantity.

◆ Confused

Confused as a goat on AstroTurf.

My tongue got caught in my eye teeth, and I couldn't see what
   I was saying.

I can explain it to you, but I can't understand it for you.

Cattywampus to Miss Jones's.

Seven ways to sundown.

See also Inept.

Coward

See Scared.

Crazy

Her phone's off the hook.

He don't know if he's a-washing
  or a-hanging.

He's got a big hole in his screen door.

She's one bubble off plumb.

She's one brick shy of a load.

She's a couple of sandwiches shy of a picnic.

She came right off the spool.

She stays upstairs.

He's a few pickles short of a barrel.

He's not playing with a full deck [*also means "dishonest"*].

"Her phone's off the hook."

He doesn't have both oars in the water.

She doesn't know if she's shucking or shelling.

He lost too many balls in the high weeds.

He's missing a few buttons off his shirt.

He's not firing on all four cylinders.

He's lost his vertical hold.

He's overdrawn at the memory bank.

She's got too many cobwebs in the attic.

His elevator doesn't go all the way
to the top.

There's a light or two burned out on his
string.

The porch light's on but no one's home.

Asleep at the wheel [also means
"incompetent" or "stupid"].

Crazy as a bullbat.

"He's lost his vertical hold."

Crazy as a bedbug.

Crazy as a betsy-bug.

Crazy as Larrabee's calf.

Crazy as a fundamentalist on
　　firewater.

Goofy as a barnyard owl.

Goofy as a road lizard.

I hear you clucking, but I can't find your nest.

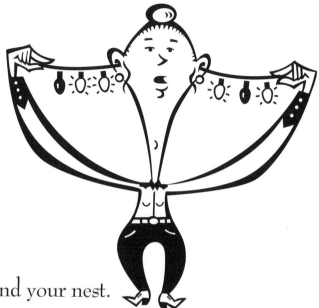

"There's a light or two burned out
on his string."

Dark

Dark as the inside of a wolf.

Dark as coffin air.

Dark as a pocket.

Dark as a crow.

Dark as crude.

Dark as the devil's riding boots.

Dark as truckstop coffee.

Black as a blue norther.

Dead

Dead as a peeled egg.

Dead as jerky.

Dead as a doornail.

Buzzard bait.

The buzzards are circling.

He gave up his guitar for a harp.

He ate a bitter pill.

She opened herself up a worm farm.

She's fertilizing the fields.

She's dead; she just won't lie down.

Her candle's been snuffed.

His picture went dark.

The devil's comin' round with his bill.

Departure, Completion

Let's light a shuck [or *"light a rag"*].

Let's blow this pop stand.

Let's skip this fleapit.

Let's absquatulate.

It's time to heat up the bricks.

It's time to put the chairs in the wagon.

It's time to put the tools on the truck.

It's time to swap spit and hit the road.

It's time to put out the fire and call in the dogs.

He's heading for the wagon yard.

He turkey-tailed it for home.

That about puts the rag on the bush.

That's all she wrote.

We're off like a dirty shirt.

We're off like sour milk.

We're off like a jug handle.

We'uns been, you'uns come.

Got to go kill a chicken and churn [*also means "busy"*].

Let's take to the tall timber.

I about have all the rabbits in a corner.

Git along, little dogies.

Come see us.

Y'all come back [*or just "y'all come"*].

Y'all hold down the fort.

The train's leavin' the station.

Church is out.

Desolate

Looks like hell with everyone out to lunch.

Out where the buses don't run.

Forty miles to wood, twenty miles to water, ten miles to hell.

They lived so far out in the country that the sun set between their house and town.

It's been pretty quiet out here since the buffalo died.

A gone-yonder country.

Difficult

Like trying to bag flies.

Like putting socks on a rooster.

Harder than picking up sticks with your butt cheeks.

That's a long hard row to hoe.

Dishonest

He's on a first-name basis with the bottom of the deck.

He'd steal the cross from a church.

There are a lot of nooses in his family tree.

There are liars, damn liars, and politicians.

They'd rather cheat you out of it than have you give it to them for free.

He's more crooked than a cowbird.

He's so crooked that if he swallowed a nail he'd spit up a corkscrew.

She's so crooked you can't tell from her tracks if she's coming or going.

He's so crooked he has to unscrew his britches at night.

He's so crooked he meets himself coming home.

He knows more ways to take your money than a roomful of lawyers.

She lies like a tombstone.

Her promises are like pie crust—easily broken.

He's a slant-hole driller.

He's a ring-tailed rounder.

He's a skunk-oil salesman.

Like pinto beans, she'll talk behind your back.

Lower than a mole's belly button on digging day.

Lower than flea skis.

Crooked as a dog's hind leg.

Crooked as the Brazos.

Crooked as a barrel of fish hooks.

Queer as a three-dollar bill.

Greasy as fried lard.

Slicker than a slop jar.

Slicker than a boiled onion.

Slicker than a greased pig.

Slicker than deer guts on a doorknob.

Slicker than oilcloth.

Slicker than cellophane.

More twists than a pretzel factory.

I don't trust him any farther than I can throw him.

See also Bad.

Distance

Down the road a piece.

A fur piece.

Turn left past yonder.

Two hoots and a holler away.

From here to there and back again.

I won't say it's far, but I had to grease the wagon twice before I hit the main road.

I won't say it's far, but you better pack the pantry.

The sun has riz, the sun has set, and here I is, in Texas yet
   [*vintage postcard sentiment*].

Drunk

Drunkulent.

Drunk as a fiddler's bitch.

Drunk as Cooter Brown.

Drunk as a barn weasel [*or a meadow mouse*].

High as the Piney Woods.

Snot-slinging drunk.

Owl-eyed and fish-gilled.

So drunk he couldn't hit the ground with his hat in three throws.

So drunk he couldn't see a hole in a ladder.

So drunk he can't scratch himself.

So drunk he can't pull his hand from his pocket.

Drunker than who shot John.

Drunker than a boiled owl.

She's been thumped over the head with Samson's jawbone
 [a *hangover*].

He's got the whistlebelly thumps and skull cramps [a *hangover*].

Don't chop any wood tonight, Daddy's coming home with a load.

He wasn't born, just squeezed out of a bartender's rag.

He's got calluses on his elbows.

Calling for Earl [*or Ralph, or Ruth: throwing up*].

He foreswore his Fritos [*threw up*].

He laughed at the linoleum [*threw up*].

Jugging and jawing.

You got her drunk, you take her home.

Commode-hugging, knee-walking, falling-down drunk.

Stewed as prunes.

She's been brown-bagging it since her cradle days.

She's been lapping in the gutter.

He's been talking to the devil and dead men.

He's got the gravel rash.

He's been among the Philistines.

She has a guest in the attic.

Let's drown some bourbon.

We were overserved all night long.

See also Cheap; Immoral.

Dry

Dry as a powder house.

Drier than the heart of a haystack.

The creek's so low we've started hauling water *to* it.

It's been dry so long, we only got a quarter-inch of rain during Noah's flood.

"So dry I'm spitting cotton."

So dry I'm spitting cotton.

So dry the fish are carrying canteens.

So dry the trees are bribing the dogs.

So dry my duck don't know how to swim.

So dry the Baptists are sprinkling, the Methodists are spitting, and the Catholics are giving rain checks.

It's so dry the birds are building their nests out of barbed wire.

Dull

(as a knife)

It wouldn't cut hot butter.

You could scratch your back with it and never draw blood.

You might as well give it to Baby for a plaything.

You could ride all the way to Big Spring on it and never
split a hair.

Dull

(boring)

As exciting as a mashed-potato sandwich.

As much fun as chopping wood.

As much fun as sitting around watching the grass grow.

As much fun as sitting around watching paint dry.

Dull as Henry's hoe.

Dumb

If a duck had his brain, it would fly north for the winter.

If he was bacon, he wouldn't even sizzle.

If brains were leather, he couldn't saddle a flea.

If all her brains were ink, she couldn't dot an *i*.

If all her brains were dynamite, she couldn't blow her nose.

If he had a brain, it'd die of loneliness.

If dumb was dirt, he'd cover about an acre.

She was behind the door when the brains were passed out.

He carries his brains in his back pocket.

She's got a single-digit I.Q.

She's a little short behind the ears.

She hasn't got the sense God gave little green apples.

He owns a twenty-dollar horse and a hundred-dollar saddle.

Sharp as a mashed potato.

Dumb as dirt.

Dumb as a stump.

Dumb as a box of rocks.

Dumb as a bar ditch.

Dumb as a barrel of hair.

Dumb as a wagon wheel.

Dumb as a prairie dog.

Dumb as a watermelon.

Dumb enough for twins.

He doesn't know "come here" from "sic 'em."

He's doesn't know cain't from ain't.

He don't know nothing from nothing.

He doesn't know a widget from a whangdoodle.

He don't know diddly squat.

He don't know pooh turkey.

"If brains were leather, he couldn't saddle a flea."

39

She doesn't have enough sense to spit downwind.

She doesn't know enough to pound sand down a rat hole.

She doesn't know enough to keep beans out of chili.

She doesn't know any more than the man in the moon.

She doesn't know beans about it.

She doesn't know which end's up.

She knows more about that than a hog does about Sunday.

He can't ride and chew at the same time.

He went to Cowpatty College.

So dumb he'd hold a fish underwater
   to drown it.

**"So stupid if you put his
brains in a bumblebee, it
would fly backwards."**

So stupid if you put his brains in a bumblebee, it would fly backwards.

So thick-headed you can hit him in the face with a tire iron and he won't yell till morning.

Her head drains faster than a bathtub.

She could screw up an anvil.

He couldn't track a wagon through a mud puddle.

He couldn't find his butt with a flashlight in each hand.

He couldn't pour rain out of a boot with a hole in the toe and directions on the heel.

He's not the sharpest knife in the drawer.

Easy

No hill for a stepper.

Slick as a whistle.

Easy as breaking eggs.

Easy as falling off a log.

Easy as sipping cider.

Easy as picking your nose.

A milk run [*also means "prolonged"*].

Everything

The whole kit and caboodle.

The whole shootin' match.

The whole shebang.

The whole nine yards.

Everything but the kitchen sink.

Everything but the broody hen.

Everything but the hair, horns, and holler.

Right down to a gnat's bristle.

Money, marbles, and chalk.

Exclamations

Come hell or high water.

Lord willing and the creek don't rise.

Bless your little cotton socks!

What in the Sam Hill . . . ?

Boy howdy!

Hold her, boys, she's heading for the pea patch!

Root, hog, or die!

Go like stink!

Dadgum it!

Hell's bells!

Calf rope! [*I surrender.*]

Strap it on 'em like a gas mask!

I mean to shout!

I hope to shout!

For cryin' out loud!

I don't care if it harelips the governor.

Dog me if I'll do it.

Dog bite my buttons!

The devil and Tom Walker!

Gosh-all hemlock!

44 I'll be there if nothing breaks or comes untwisted.

I'll be jiggered.

I'll be switched.

I'll be dipped.

I'll be go to hell.

That'll blow your skirt up.

That'll nip your wick.

That'll blow your hat in the creek.

That'll rip the rag right off your bush.

Am I right, or Amarillo?

If that was a snake, it would've bit you.

When it gets right down to the nut-cutting . . .

When it gets right down to the lick-log . . .

When it gets right down to the nitty-gritty . . .

When stoop comes to grunt . . .

Well, cut off my legs and call me Shorty!

Well, eat my lunch and call me hungry!

Well, slap my mama!

Well, don't that beat all!

Well, I'll be!

Well, I swan!

Katie, bar the door!

See also Insults.

Expensive

Spendy.

Higher than a cat's back.

Higher than a city skirt.

Higher than a buzzard.

As pricey as picture-show popcorn.

As dear as oysters.

Too rich for my blood.

Failure

She blames everything on the weather or her raising.

He got caught in his own loop.

He came close to the dollar knife.

He's just an ol' used-to-be.

She took her ducks to a poor market.

It went south.

Close, but no cigar.

See also Beat; Inept.

Fast

Any faster and she'd catch up to yesterday.

He can blow out the lamp and jump into bed before it gets dark.

He gets there in one-half less than no time.

He high-tailed it out of there.

"Any faster and she'd catch up to yesterday."

Movin' like he was goin' for the doctor.

Quicker than hell could scorch a feather.

Quick out of the chute.

Quick as a hiccup.

Faster than small-town gossip.

Faster than a prairie fire with a tail wind.

Faster than a scalded cat.

Faster than greased lightning.

Faster than double-struck lightning.

Faster than a sneeze through a screen door.

Faster than moonshine through a tow sack.

Faster than a dust devil.

Lickety-split.

Quicker than God could get the news.

Going like a house afire.

"Quicker than God
could get the news."

Hell-bent for leather.

In a New York minute.

Food, Hunger

Hungrier than a woodpecker with a headache.

Hungrier than a hibernating bear.

Hungrier than a bitch wolf with seventeen pups.

I'm so hungry I could eat the south end of a northbound
nanny goat.

I'm so hungry I could eat a jackrabbit, ears and all.

I'm having a sinking spell [*also means "tired"*].

My belly and my backbone are bumpin'.

She fixed enough to feed Coxey's army.

She rustled up some grub.

It's larrupin' good.

It's soppin' good.

Good enough to lap a lip over.

So good it'll make childbirth a pleasure.

So good it'll make you want to dance naked.

I'm full as a tick.

I'm full as an egg.

I'm suffering with comfort.

I'm feeling peckish.

Let's surround some grub.

Tastes like stump water [*said of bad coffee*].

Let your vittles stop your mouth. ["*Let's eat!*"]

Foolish

See Inept.

Friendship

The porch light is always burning.

Long as I got a biscuit, you got half.

He'd lend you his last pair of longjohns.

She brings a cup of sugar when she comes calling.

General Advice

Never sign nothing by neon.

Never call a man a liar because he knows more than you do.

There never was a horse that couldn't be rode or a rider who couldn't be throwed.

Just because a chicken has wings don't mean it can fly.

Chicken one day; feathers the next.

Today's butcher is tomorrow's beef.

A squeaky wheel gets the grease, but a quacking duck gets shot.

A pat on the back don't cure saddle sores.

A monkey in silk is still a monkey.

A worm is the only animal that can't fall down.

A loose horse always seeks new pastures.

The wilder the colt, the finer the horse.

The wolf loses his teeth, not his nature.

Kicking never gets you nowhere, unless you're a mule.

It's better to pull your weight than your gun.

It takes more to plow a field than turning it over in your mind.

It'll never show on a galloping horse.

It's time to paint your butt white and run with the antelope.

It's better to die on your feet than live on your knees.

You can't slop sprinklers and dippers at the same trough
   [a *religious reference*].

You can't get lard unless you boil the hog.

You can't stomp a snake with both feet in the bucket.

You can't fry beans without lard.

If you don't like the barking, throw a sop to the dogs.

If you cut your own firewood, it'll warm you twice.

If a frog had wings, he wouldn't bump his ass a-hoppin'.

If the saddle creaks, it's not paid for.

If you lie down with dogs, you get up with fleas.

If you run with the wolves, learn how to howl.

If you can't run with the big dogs, stay on the porch.

There's never a good time to have your gun jam.

There's more than one way to skin a cat.

There's more than one way to break a dog from sucking eggs.

There's a big difference between the ox and the whiffletree.

There's no tree but bears some fruit.

Give me the bacon without the sizzle.

Give him an inch, he'll take a mile—and you'll pay the freight.

Pigs get fat; hogs get slaughtered.

Everyone has his own way of killing fleas.

Let bygones be bygones, but remember the Alamo.

Don't try to teach your grandma to milk mice.

"Don't squat on your spurs."

Don't toss your rope before you loop it.

Don't hang your wash on someone else's line.

Don't whistle what should be sung.

Don't squat on your spurs.

Don't wet on my leg and tell me it's raining.

Do your Texas best.

Dance with the one that brung you.

Men and barbed wire have their good points.

A guilty fox hunts his own hole.

Don't rile the wagon master.

No use winking at a pretty girl in a dark room.

Better to keep your mouth shut and seem a fool, than to open it and remove all doubt.

The bigger the mouth, the better it looks when shut.

A closed mouth catches no flies.

The cowboy that straddles the fence gets a sore crotch.

Skin your own buffalo.

Clean your own catfish.

Any mule's tail can catch cockleburs.

A drought usually ends with a flood.

A lean dog runs fast.

A wink's as good as a smile to a blind mule.

The apple doesn't fall far from the tree.

Only a fool argues with a skunk, a mule, or a cook.

Man is the only animal that can be skinned more than once.

With poison, one drop is enough.

Even the best horse needs to be spurred.

For the man destined to become a tamale, corn shucks will fall from heaven.

One visits the cactus only when it bears fruit.

See also Miscellaneous.

Good, Happy

Sweeter than stolen honey.

Sweeter than baby's breath.

Sweeter than an old maid's dreams.

He took to you like a hog to persimmons.

She took to you like sticker burrs to bare feet.

"Happy as a clam at high tide."

Happy as a boardinghouse pup.

Happy as a clam at high tide.

Happy as a hog in mud.

Happy as a hog in slops.

Safe as Granny's snuff box.

Fair to middling.

Pert as a cricket.

Clean as a coon.

Fat and sassy.

All sweetness and light.

Mannerable.

I'm cooking with gas.

I'm cooking on a front burner today.

Bright-eyed and bushy-tailed.

The greatest thing since sliced bread.

The greatest thing since apple butter.

If I felt any better, I'd drop my harp plumb through the cloud.

If I felt any better, I'd think it was a setup.

My spirits rose like a corncob in a cistern.

"Pert as a cricket."

It's back-scratching time at the old corral.

High, wide, and handsome.

I thought I'd died and gone to heaven.

She's got a lot of stars in her crown.

She's a real piece of work [*often used sarcastically*].

She's finer than wine and gooder than snuff.

She'd give away her head if she could unfasten it.

She dropped off of St. Peter's coat tail.

Fine as frog hair split four ways.

Fine as boomtown silk.

Fine as dollar cotton.

Fine as frog fur.

Fine as cream gravy.

**"If I felt any better,
I'd drop my harp plumb
through the cloud."**

He's such a gentleman, he gets to his feet when his wife comes in with the firewood.

He hung the sun, the moon, the stars, and a horse thief.

He's so kind he has to hire someone to kick his dog.

More fun than a packed-pew preacher.

I haven't had so much fun since Patton was a private.

I haven't had so much fun since Hector was a pup.

I haven't had so much fun since the hogs ate Sister.

I haven't had so much fun since the legs fell off Nell's hamster.

See also Friendship; Lucky.

Goodbye

See Departure.

Handsome

See Pretty.

Handy

Handy as shirt pockets.

Handy as a rope at a hanging.

Handy as a latch on the outhouse door.

Handy as hip pockets on a hog.

Happy

See Good.

Hard

Hard as a pew.

Hard as caliche.

Hard as a Baptist pallet on a parlor floor.

Harder than last night's cornbread.

Harder than a whore's heart.

See also Difficult.

Hello

See Arrival.

Honest

If that ain't a fact, I'm a possum.

If I say a hen dips snuff, you can look under her wing for the can.

If I tell you a chicken can pull a plow, you can hook it up and
    make a crop.

You can take that to the bank.

You can hang your hat on it.

You can bet the farm on it.

He's so honest you could shoot craps with him over the phone.

He sits tall in the saddle.

He totes level.

Hot

Hot as Hades.

Hot as tarnation.

Hot as the hinges of hell [or, *the hubs of hell*].

Hot as a depot stove.

Hot as a two-dollar pistol.

Hot as a summer revival.

Hot as a pot of neck bones.

Hot as a billy goat in a pepper patch.

Hot as a stolen tamale.

Hotter than whoopee in woolens.

Hotter than a honeymoon hotel.

Hotter than a preacher's knee.

Hotter than a burning stump.

Hotter than blue blazes.

"Hot as a billy goat in a pepper patch."

Hotter than a fur coat in Marfa.

Hotter than a Dutch oven with the biscuits burnin'.

Hotter than a little red wagon [*also means "successful"*].

Hot enough to fry eggs on the sidewalk.

So hot the hens are laying hard-boiled eggs.

The heat's done addled my brains.

Immoral, Wild

They call her "radio station" because anyone
   can pick her up, especially at night.

He's wilder than a peach orchard boar.

She's just naturally horizontal.

She wears her own trailer hitch.

He was all over her like ugly on an ape.

**"They call her 'radio station' because anyone can
pick her up, especially at night."**

He'll take up with any hound that'll hunt with him.

She'll wrap herself around you like a sweet-potato vine.

Loose as ashes in the wind.

Loose as a bucket of soot.

Free as fresh air.

Free as fliers.

Wilder than an acre of snakes.

She doesn't wear much more than a ring and a smile.

He was born on the wrong side of the blanket.

They ate supper before they said grace.

They planted their crop before they built their fence.

They're hitched but not churched.

They've got a cotton-patch license.

His lips ain't no prayerbook.

See also Drunk.

Inept, Useless

She could fall up a tree.

He could screw up a two-car funeral.

She couldn't ride a nightmare without falling out of bed.

She couldn't count to twenty on her fingers and toes.

He couldn't knock a hole in the wind with a sackful of hammers.

She couldn't hit the floor if she fell out of bed.

He couldn't catch a cold in the Klondike.

He couldn't get a whore a date on a troop train.

He's so bad at farming he couldn't raise Cain.

He's such a loser, he bought a suit with two pairs of pants, then burned a hole in the jacket.

She'd have to learn how to be a fool.

He isn't worth the powder and lead it would take to shoot him.

He's got no more chance than a june bug in the chicken coop.

He's worthless as wet bread.

He's not worth ten cents in Confederate money.

He doesn't know split peas from coffee.

He doesn't know gee from haw.

It looks like she sewed it with a hot needle and burnt thread.

She's like a rubber-nosed woodpecker in a petrified forest.

She's permanently snakebit.

She's like a cow's tail—always behind.

He'd fry the skillet and throw away the handle.

She's always a day late and a dollar short.

Worthless as a pitcher of warm spit.

Useless as two wagons in a one-horse town.

Useless as last year's bird nest.

Useless as a government employee.

Useless as ice trays in hell.

Useless as a knot in a stake rope.

Useless as ball moss.

Useless as a glass of hot gravy in July.

You might as well smoke rope.

He's Rexall [a *drugstore cowboy*].

Not worth spit.

No more good than an eyeless needle.

Like warming up leftover snow.

That doesn't amount to a hill of beans.

Don't just sit there like a bump on a log.

Like pushing a wheelbarrow with
    rope handles.

Like sweet-talking the water out of the well.

Tie a quarter to it and throw it away,
    and you can say you lost something.

**"He's Rexall
[a drugstore cowboy]."**

If she'd been cooking for the North, the South would have won the war.

I need that like a hog needs a sidesaddle.

I need that like a tomcat needs a trousseau.

See also Confused; Dumb; Failure.

"I need that like a tomcat needs a trousseau."

Insults, Retorts

Even a blind hog can find an acorn.

Even a blind chicken can find a kernel of corn.

Anytime you happen to pass my house, I'd sure appreciate it.

You couldn't carry a tune in a bucket with the lid nailed shut.

Go peddle your own produce.

Go cork your pistol.

Go throw your applesauce.

Go tuck in your bib.

Were you raised in a barn?

Why shear a pig?

"You couldn't carry a tune in a bucket with the lid nailed shut."

Lick that calf again?

Mind your own biscuits.

Snap your own garters.

Thank you for that crumb.

Why close the barn door after the horses are out?

Are you spoiled, or do you always smell that way?

If you think that, you've got another think coming.

If you don't like it, you can just lump it.

If you break your leg, don't come running to me.

What did you do with the money your mama gave you for
    singing lessons?

Even the chickens under the porch know *that*.

That's two different buckets of possums.

You smell like you want to be left alone.

She don't sweat much for a fat girl.

Put that in your pipe and smoke it.

If you're so smart, why aren't you rich?

Cripple that horse and walk it by me real slow.

Whatever melts your butter.

Whatever greases your wagon.

Another county heard from.

I wouldn't put him out if he was on fire.

I'll believe it when there's whales in West Texas.

See also Exclamations.

**"You smell like you
want to be left alone."**

Lazy

He hangs out more often than Mama's washing.

He's like a blister—he doesn't show up until the work's all done.

He's just standing around with his teeth in his mouth.

He'll never be in danger of drowning in sweat.

She's itching for something she won't scratch for.

She's so lazy she can't even hold her head up.

As lazy as the hound that leaned against the fence to bark.

Length

Long as a rope with just one end.

Longer than a Mormon clothesline.

Longer than the way west.

Liar

See Dishonest.

Lucky

They tried to hang him but the rope broke.

He could draw a pat hand from a stacked deck.

He always draws the best bull.

He's riding a gravy train with biscuit wheels.

She could sit on the fence and the birds would feed her.

See also Good.

"She could sit on the fence and the birds would feed her."

73

Mad

She could start a fight in an empty house.

She always reckons on a ruckus.

He'd argue with a wooden Indian.

She raised hell and stuck a chunk under it.

He's the only hell his mama ever raised.

She's the hell-raisingest woman I ever knew.

He's tearing up the pea patch.

She let me have it with both barrels.

He jumped on me like a duck on a june bug.

He jumped on me like white on rice.

She jumped on me with all four feet.

He's got his tail up.

He's filing his teeth.

She's in a horn-tossing mood.

She's in a sod-pawing mood.

She's so contrary she floats upstream.

She's dancing in the hog trough.

He'll tell you how the cow ate the cabbage [*also means* "honest"].

He'll fight with you till hell freezes over,
    then skate with you on the ice.

Mad as an old wet hen.

Mad as a cow with a sore teat.

Mad as a red ant.

I'm so mad I could stomp baby ducks.

I'm so mad I could stretch sheet iron.

I'm so mad I could eat a horny toad backwards.

I'm gonna cloud up and rain knuckles.

"I'm so mad I could stomp baby ducks."

He's spoutin' steam at every joint.

She's up on her high horse [*also means* "vain"].

She's up on her hind legs.

She had a hissy fit.

She had a conniption fit.

His didy pin must be sticking him.

He's about to blow a gasket.

He was raised on clabber.

She got all cross-legged about it.

She's in a lather.

You wouldn't be happy if they hung you with a new rope.

That really raises my hackles.

That really burns my britches.

That burns me up like a chicken at a barbecue.

Mean

See Bad.

Miscellaneous

Independent as a hog on ice.

Fancier than a two-story outhouse.

Bolder than a brass spittoon.

Calm as a horse trough.

Lively as an electric fence.

Out like Lottie's eye [asleep; *passed-out drunk*].

Naked as a jaybird.

White as a motel tan.

Brown as a berry.

Purple as a possum's posterior.

Black as sin.

Clean as a hound's tooth.

Clean as a bean in a washing machine.

Clean as a coon [*deftly done*].

Slick as a gut [*deftly done*].

Surprised as a pup with his first porcupine.

Her eyes were stickin' out like the cowcatcher on a switch engine.

I don't know him from Adam's off ox [*or, Adam's housecat*].

She stuck to it like a june bug to a screen door.

Baptists and Johnson grass are taking over.

She's still sewing for her hope chest
[*she's unmarried*].

He looks like he swallowed a horse
except for the tail [*he has a beard*].

We killed a bear—Pa shot it
[*taking undue credit*].

I saved my manners and my possum
[*said of a declined invitation*].

See also General Advice.

**"Baptists and Johnson
grass are taking over."**

Nervous

Nervous as a whore in church.

Nervous as a pregnant jenny.

Nervous as a fly in the glue jar.

Nervous as a woodshed waiter.

Jumpy as spit on a hot skillet.

Calm as a june bug.

"Nervous as a woodshed waiter."

Shaking like a cloth in the wind [*also means "drunk"*].

Running like a sage hen.

Bouncing around like a huckleberry on a wagon bed.

Like a wiggletail in hot ashes.

She's so nervous she has to thread her sewing machine while it's running.

She's chewing her bit.

He makes a pressure cooker look calm.

He'd worry the warts off a frog.

He won't stand hitched.

He's grinning like a mule eating cockleburs.

He's grinning like a pig eating persimmons.

"He's grinning like a mule eating cockleburs."

Noisy

Noisy as two skeletons dancing on a tin roof.

Noisy as a restless mule in a tin barn.

Noisy as white trash at a tent meeting.

Noisier than cats making kittens.

Noisier than a cornhusk mattress.

Louder than Grandpa's Sunday tie.

He called his hogs all night [*he snored*].

He learned to whisper in a sawmill.

Dogie-loud.

"He called his hogs all night [he snored]."

Old

Old as Methuselah.

Old as water.

Old as dirt.

Old as Arbuckle's [*a nineteenth-century coffee brand*].

Since Hector was a pup.

Evenings are cooler than mornings.

He's back on oatmeal.

He's been around since who laid the chunk.

She's been around since before water was wet.

She was around when the Dead Sea was only sick.

She's living on God's sense of humor.

He's getting along in years, but his horns ain't been sawed off yet.

He's so old he keeps his own buzzards.

Over

See Departure; Completion.

Patience

Don't get your panties in a wad.

Don't get all het up about it.

Hot will cool if greedy will let it.

Take a tater and wait.

Keep your shirt on [or, *your pants on*].

Wash off your war paint.

It'll come around on the gi-tar.

See also General Advice.

Poor

If a trip around the world cost a dollar, I couldn't get to the
Oklahoma line.

Broker than the Ten Commandments.

Broker than a stick horse.

Poor as a lizard-eating cat.

Poor as sawmill rats.

Poor as Job's turkey.

Can't make tongue and buckle meet.

She lives on the other side of across the tracks.

I ate so many armadillos when I was young, I still roll up into a ball when I hear a dog bark.

I'm so broke I couldn't buy hay for a nightmare.

So poor I had a tumbleweed for a pet.

So poor we had to fertilize the sills before we could raise the windows.

So poor we can't go window shopping.

So poor the bank won't let me draw breath.

So poor I can't pay attention.

So poor all she has to her name is a Butterick pattern dress.

So poor the wolf won't even stop at their door.

So poor their Sunday supper is fried water.

Too poor to paint, too proud to whitewash.

All he owns is the shirt on his back, and the buttons are on account.

He's bent but not broke.

He's been hard-wintered.

You're liable to hear anything at their house but the jingling of change and the frying of bacon.

It's no sin to be poor—but it's damned inconvenient.

Pregnant

She's got a bun in the oven.

She's sitting on the nest.

She's got one in the chute.

She's been storked.

Pretty, Handsome

I'd rather watch her walk than eat fried chicken.

She can ride any horse in my string.

She's built like a brick outhouse.

She's shapelier than a Coke bottle.

She cleans up real nice.

She has more curves than a barrel of snakes.

She's all dressed up like a country bride [or *a gambler's bride*].

He's all dressed up like a sore thumb.

She's purely ornamental.

She catches your eye like a tin roof on a sunny day.

So pretty she'd make a man plow through a stump.

So pretty you can drink her coffee anyway.

Pretty as twelve acres of pregnant red hogs.

Pretty as a red heifer in a flower bed.

Pretty as a pie supper.

Pretty as dollar cotton.

Cute as a calico kitten on down south.

Cute as a speckled pup under a red wagon.

Cute as kitten pajamas.

He's a long tall drink of water.

He's handsome as a handful of spades.

See also Good.

Problem, Trouble

The barn door's open and the mule's trying
   to run [*your fly's down*].

The cattle are getting mighty thirsty.

There's a big hole in the fence.

There's a dead cat on the line.

There are weevils in the flour sack.

There's a yellowjacket in the outhouse.

That horse is heading home with an
   empty saddle.

"The barn door's open
and the mule's trying to
run [your fly's down]."

My ox is getting gored.

We're up a creek without a canoe.

We've got to dodge that bullet.

He's sucking for a bruise.

He loaded the wrong wagon.

He ripped his britches.

I got my ox in a ditch.

I got to drain that swamp.

I've got my tail in a crack.

They hung the wrong
horse thief.

Time to circle the wagons.

Time to get the hell out
of Dodge.

**"There's a yellowjacket
in the outhouse."**

That's where the mule throwed Russell.

Things are going to hell in a handbasket around here.

Quantity

A passel.

A sight.

A heap.

A clutch.

A slew.

A chance.

Umpteen.

"We've got to dodge that bullet."

More than you can shake a stick at.

More than Carter has pills.

More than Quaker has oats.

More than Van Camp's has beans.

See also Common.

Quiet

So quiet you could have heard a rat cough.

Quiet as a Quaker meeting.

Quiet as death.

Rare

See Scarce.

Rich

In tall cotton [or, *in high cotton*].

Running with the big dogs [*also means "powerful"*].

He's one of the big-hat boys.

She's got more than she can say grace over.

She's got more money than a porcupine has quills.

She took rich from her mama and daddy.

Rich enough to eat her laying hens.

Rich as feedlot dirt.

Rich as Daisy Bradford.

We're keeping the wolves away.

He butters his bread on both sides.

They didn't come to town two to a mule.

So rich they can eat fried chicken all week long.

God gives money to the wealthy so they won't starve.

Sad, Unfortunate

I feel lower than a gopher hole.

I feel so low I couldn't jump off a dime.

She eats sorrow by the spoonful.

You look like you were sent for and couldn't go.

He looks like the cheese fell off his cracker.

Sad enough to bring a tear to a glass eye.

He's the moaningfullest person I ever did see.

She wails like a new widow.

I'm bluer than the Panhandle sky.

I'm blue as a norther.

I've got a rare case of the mullygrubs.

I'm all cut up like a boardinghouse pie.

Jinxed as Jonah.

Scarce, Rare

Scarce as hen's teeth.

Scarce as grass around a hog trough.

Scarce as rain barrels.

Rare as a fair jury.

Rare as an honest lawyer.

Rare as a poor politician.

Scared, Shy

Scared as a cat at the dog pound.

Scared as a sinner in a cyclone.

He stays in the shadow of his mama's apron.

He's first cousin to Moses Rose.

He's yellow as mustard but without the bite.

He may not be a chicken, but he has his
henhouse ways.

He backed out quicker than a crawfish.

If he was melted down, he couldn't
be poured into a fight.

She wouldn't bite a biscuit.

Yellow suits her.

He's whistling past the graveyard.

He's trembling in his boots.

"He may not be a chicken, but
he has his henhouse ways."

It scared the pudding out of me.

Shy as a mail-order bride.

Shy as a crocus.

Shy as sapphires.

Shy as unshucked corn.

Lily-livered.

Whey-faced.

I feel like a possum trotted
over my grave.

"Shy as a mail-order bride."

Serious

Serious as the business end of a .45.

Serious as polio [*or cancer, or a stroke*].

Serious as an undertaker.

Serious as a TV preacher.

Shy

See Scared.

Sick

He's got a hitch in his gitalong.

He's all stove up.

Her hopper's busted.

She looks like death warmed over.

I'm so sick I'd have to get better to die.

I feel tore down almost level to the ground.

I've got the green apple nasties.

It ouches me something fierce.

Pitiful as a three-legged dog.

Sore as a boil.

Sore as a tenderfoot's tail.

Sick as a dog passing peach pits.

So sick he needs two beds.

Too sick to drink and too thin to plow.

As full of pains as an old window.

Green around the gills.

See also Tired.

Slow

He's so slow he could gain weight walking.

She's so slow she fell off the bed and didn't hit the floor till morning.

Slow as molasses.

Slow as Christmas.

Slow as Grandma Moses.

Slower than Grandma Turtle.

Small, Thin

She wears her bra backwards and it fits.

She's frying size.

She's poor as a rail fence.

He's knee-high to a grasshopper.

He'd have to stand up to look a rattler in the eye.

About as big as the little end of nothing.

Half as big as a minute.

No bigger than moles on a chigger.

Short as pie crust.

Not as big as a bar of soap after a day's washing.

Scrawny as Ace Reid cattle.

Nothing between the horns and hooves but hide.

No higher than a shirt pocket.

Thin as a bat's ear.

Thin as a gnat's whisker.

Thin as store-bought thread.

Thin as Depression soup.

Thin as a fiddle string.

Thin as a rake and twice as sexy.

Lean as a longhorn.

Lean as a lodgepole.

Flat as a fritter.

Scarce-hipped.

So skinny she has to stand twice to make a shadow.

So skinny you could give her a Big Red and use her as a thermometer.

So skinny she shades herself under the clothesline.

So skinny his belt buckle rubbed a sore on his backbone.

It's just a wide spot in the road [said of a town].

Smart

Bright as a new penny.

Smart as a hooty owl.

Smart as a whip.

She's got a mind like a steel trap.

She's a walking encyclopedia.

He's deep as the Piney Woods.

He's deep as a slough.

There's no flies on my mama.

Sharper than a pocketful of toothpicks.

It don't take him long to look at a horseshoe.

See also Capable.

Soft

Soft as a two-minute egg.

Soft as a young calf's ears.

Soft as a señorita's skin.

Soft as blackstrap molasses.

Soft [or *smooth*] as satin [or *silk*].

Speed

See Fast.

Strong

His breath's so strong you could hang out the wash on it.

His breath's so strong it could light the stove.

Strong as acky-forty [a *reference to aquafortis, the old-fashioned name for nitric acid*].

Strong as an ox.

Strong as Samson.

Stronger than moonshine.

Stronger than a garlic milkshake.

Bull-stout.

That coffee's so strong it'll put hair on your chest.

That coffee's so strong it'll raise a blood blister on a boot.

That coffee's so strong it'll walk into your cup.

He's so strong he makes Samson look sensitive.

He's so strong he could make a Texas Ranger cry.

Stubborn

Hame-headed.

Stubborn as a splinter.

Stubborn as a scar.

Stubborn as mesquite.

Stubborn as a mule in clover.

He'll stick to it like an East Texas chigger.

He's deaf in one ear and can't hear out of the other.

She's got no more reason than a stone.

Stupid

See Dumb.

Talkative

She could talk a coon right out of a tree.

He could talk the legs off a chair.

He could talk the gate off its hinges.

He could talk the hide off a cow.

He could talk the ears off a mule.

She could talk the horns off a billy goat.

He shoots his mouth off so much he must eat bullets for breakfast.

He's got a ten-gallon mouth.

She speaks ten words a second, with gusts to fifty.

She's a dry-hole gusher.

Her tongue is plumb tuckered.

She's got tongue enough for ten rows of teeth.

He blew in on his own wind.

He's a live dictionary.

He's a chin musician.

"She speaks ten words a second, with gusts to fifty."

She has a bell clapper instead of a tongue.

He was vaccinated with a Victrola needle.

She talks so much that when she dies, they'll have to take a stick and beat her tongue to death.

She's harvesting a bumper crop of words.

Thin

See Small.

Tight

See Cheap; Drunk.

Time

Longer than a month of Sundays.

Longer than a wet week.

From can't see to can't see [or, *from can't to can't*].

From hell to breakfast.

I spent a year there one day.

They've been married so long, they're on their third bottle of Tabasco.

See also Old.

Tired

She looks like she's been chewed up, spit out, and stepped on [*also means "ugly"*].

She looks like she was rode hard and put away wet.

She looks like chewed twine.

He looks like Bowser's bone.

His eyes look like two burn holes in a mattress.

Her eyes look like cherries in the snow.

He's panting like a lizard on a hot rock.

She's plumb tuckered out.

I'm more wore out than a flour-sack dress.

I was born tired and I've since suffered a relapse.

I'm holding myself together with both hands.

I'm near about past going.

I'm so tired I knocked a hole in my chest with my chin.

I'm so tired I could sleep on a barbed-wire fence.

I feel like the tail end of pea time.

My tongue's hanging out a foot and forty inches.

My dogs are barkin'.

One wheel down and the axle dragging.

Tired as a boomtown whore.

All lathered up like he's waiting for a shave.

See also Sick.

Trouble

See Problem.

Truthful

See Honest.

Ugly

She's so ugly she'd make a freight train take a dirt road.

She's so ugly she'd curdle the soup.

He's so ugly he'd scare the maggots off a gut wagon.

He's so ugly his cooties have to close their eyes.

He looks like he was inside the outhouse when
the lightning struck.

He looks like he was shot out of a cannon
and missed the net.

He looks like the dogs have been keepin'
him under the porch.

"He looks like he was inside the
outhouse when the lightning
struck."

She looks like she was born downwind of the outhouse.

She looks like she fell face-down in the sticker patch and the cows ran over her.

"So ugly she has to sneak up on a glass of water."

He looks like he was dragged through hell backwards and beat with buzzard guts.

So ugly the tide wouldn't take her out.

So ugly his mama had to tie a pork chop around his neck so the dogs would play with him.

So ugly his mama takes him everywhere she goes so she doesn't have to kiss him goodbye.

So ugly only his mama loves him—and she waits till payday.

So ugly his mama wore blinders when he nursed.

So ugly she has to sneak up on a glass of water.

So ugly she has to slap her feet to make them go to bed with her.

So ugly that when he was born, the doctor slapped his mama.

So ugly his face would stop an eight-day clock.

So ugly he could hold up a five-day rain.

He got whipped with an ugly stick.

His mama had more hair in the mole on her chin.

He looks like he was pulled through a knothole backwards.

She looks like ten miles of bad road.

He looks like he sorts bobcats for a living.

She's so bucktoothed she could eat corn through a picket fence.

He's so bowlegged he couldn't catch a pig in a ditch.

He's so cross-eyed he can stand up in the middle of the week and see two Sundays.

He's so freckled he looks like he swallowed a quarter and broke out in pennies.

Freckled as a guinea egg.

Wall-eyed as a frog.

Jimmy-jawed as a bulldog.

Hog-ugly.

Ugly as a mud fence.

Ugly as homemade sin.

Ugly as homemade soap.

Ugly as Grandpa's toenails.

He's got a face like the back end of bad luck.

She can't help being ugly, but she could stay home.

He couldn't get a date at the Chicken Ranch with a truckload
   of fryers.

I wouldn't take her to a dog show even if she had a chance
   of winning.

If I've got to have me a mole, I want a nice long hair right in
   the middle of it.

I look like the wrath of God.

He's got lovin' eyes—they're always looking at one another.

Her eyes look like tomatoes in a glass of buttermilk.

Her teeth are like the stars—they come out at night.

She's got skin like cream and a face like clabber.

She could bite through bacon without greasing a gum.

She's got a face long enough to eat oats out of a churn.

She's got a great face for radio.

She's got a face like an unmade bed.

Unacceptable

Not what I had my face fixed for.

Like hugging a rose bush.

Nothing to write home about.

That dog won't hunt.

That really sticks in my craw.

I'd just as soon bite a bug.

I'd rather pick cockleburs out of a skunk's rear end.

I'd rather be covered with honey and staked out over an ant bed.

I'd rather chew tin foil.

I'd rather roughhouse with a Texas Ranger.

I'd rather play leap frog with a unicorn.

I'd rather run over a skunk.

I'd rather slide down a banister of razors into a tub of alcohol.

I'd rather sleep on sandpaper.

I'd rather eat peas without pork.

I'd wouldn't have him if his head was strung with gold.

I don't cotton to it.

Step on it before it starts crawling.

See also Failure.

Unsophisticated

She just fell off the turnip [watermelon, tater] truck.

He's so country he thinks a seven-course meal is a possum and a six-pack.

I've been to two county fairs and a goat-roping, and I ain't never seen nothing like it.

He's crude as new oil.

She's country as cow chips.

Unwelcome

As welcome as an egg-sucking dog.

As welcome as an outhouse breeze.

As welcome as screwworm.

As welcome as a skunk at a lawn party.

As welcome as a wet shoe.

As welcome as a tornado on a trail drive.

As welcome as a train wreck.

As welcome as cold hands to a milk cow.

As welcome as a drunk at a revival.

As popular as a frog in the guacamole.

As popular as a porcupine at a nudist colony.

See also Bad.

Useless
See Inept.

Vain

He broke his arm patting himself on the back.

He's struttin' his okra [*showing off*].

He thinks the sun comes up just to hear him crow.

She sure is biggety.

I'd like to buy him for what he's worth and sell him for what he thinks he'd bring.

She's so spoiled salt couldn't save her.

She's so spoiled she expects spoon-feeding.

She's got more airs than an Episcopalian.

If she gets to heaven, she'll ask to see the upstairs.

He cares about nothing except Saturday night and payday.

I wish I'd been born rich instead of so damned good-looking.

See also Boastful.

"He thinks the sun comes up just to hear him crow."

Warning

See Caution.

Wasting Time

Preaching to the choir.

Just ratting around.

Burning daylight.

Burning green wood for kindling.

Beating the devil around the stump.

Arguing with a wooden Indian.

Closing the barn door after the mule is out.

Whistling up the wind.

Hollering down a well.

Hollering down the rain barrel.

Fadoodling.

He's soap-tracked [spinning his wheels].

He's bailing out his boat with a spoon.

He's wolfin' round the pot.

She's chasing a hawk's shadow.

See also Lazy.

Weak

Weak as well water.

Weak as cafe chili.

Limp as a lap-baby.

That man's so weak, a two-year-old could tump him over.

That coffee's so weak, I had to help it out of the pot.

Wealthy

See Rich.

Weather

So foggy the birds are walking.

So dusty, the rabbits are digging holes six feet in the air.

Panhandle rain [*a dust storm*].

The wind's blowing like perfume through a prom.

Looks like it's going to clabber up and rain.

It's so windy the thermometer's horizontal.

It's so windy we're using a log chain instead of a wind sock.

"So foggy the birds are walking."

It's so windy it'd blow the latch right off the door.

It's right airish out.

It's fixin' to come one.

Windier than a fifty-pound bag of whistling lips.

Nice night for a tornado.

Texas has four seasons: drought, flood, blizzard, and twister.

A real gully-washer toad-strangler [a *severe rainstorm*].

The devil's beating his wife with a frying pan [*simultaneous rain and sunshine*].

See also Hot; Cold; Dry.

Wise

See Capable; Smart.

Worthless

See Inept.

Young

Full of sass and vinegar.

Green as guacamole.

Green as a gourd.

Green as fresh firewood.

He hasn't shed his first skin.

He's between grass and hay.

He's climbing up fool's hill.

Total: 1,404

☆☆☆That's all she wrote!☆☆☆

More Laughs from gpc Gulf Publishing Company

How to Be Texan
Michael Hicks

Whether you're a Yankee, a Southerner, or a Texas native, this outrageous bestseller is the ideal guide to Texans.
66 pages, illustrations, paperback.
ISBN 0-932012-21-3   #0221   **$8.95**

Lone Star Zodiac
David Westheimer
Illustrations by Karen Westheimer

Living in Texas causes people to evolve from their personalities in the traditional zodiac to their more natural forms in the Lone Star Zodiac. All 12 signs are expressively illustrated in full color.
1995. 32 pages, full color, 7½" x 5⅛" paperback.
ISBN 0-88415-452-1   #5452   **$5.95**

The Truth About Texas
Anne Dingus

Sets straight more than 200 myths, legends, and general Texas misinformation.
1995. 190 pages, bibliography, 5³⁄₁₆" x 8¼" paperback.
ISBN 0-87719-282-0   #9282   **$9.95**

Cowboy Tales
Featuring the Debut of Hank the Cowdog!
John R. Erickson

These hilarious short stories reflect on the trials and tribulations of a Texas cowboy. This book introduces the star of Erickson's acclaimed series, Hank the Cowdog, in "Confessions of a Cowdog."
96 pages, 5½" x 8½" paperback.
ISBN 0-87719-257-X   #9257   **$6.95**

Cowboys Are Old Enough To Know Better
John R. Erickson

In this collection, Erickson writes of cowboys, horses, cattle, dogs, kids, pranks, and roping a fiberglass horse in the Library of Congress.
104 pages, 5½" x 8½" paperback.
ISBN 0-87719-256-1   #9256   **$6.95**

Cowboys Are Partly Human
John R. Erickson

A cowboy's best friend is his chiropractor. And that explains why cowboys walk funny. This and many other hilarious truths await you in twenty-two of Erickson's best short pieces on cowboy life.
100 pages, 5½" x 8½" paperback.
ISBN 0-9608612-4-6   #6124   **$6.95**

Cowboys Are a Separate Species
John R. Erickson

Witty and often reflective, each Erickson piece is an entertaining look at the world through the unique perspective of a High Plains cowboy.
96 pages, 5½" x 8½" paperback.
ISBN 0-916941-18-3   #4118   **$6.95**

Visit Your Favorite Bookstore!

Or order directly from:
Gulf Publishing Company
P.O. Box 2608 • Dept. IC
Houston, Texas 77252-2608
713-520-4444 • FAX: 713-525-4647

Send payment plus $4.95 ($6.15 if the order is $20 or more, $7.75 for orders of $30 or more) shipping and handling or credit card information. CA, IL, NJ, PA, and TX residents must add sales tax on books and shipping total. Price and availability subject to change without notice.

Thank you for your order!